The
Power
of
Ownership

The
Power
of
Ownership

A tale about the importance of taking
control of your career and your life.

MICHAEL D. KHOURI

A D PROFESSIONAL DEVELOPMENT PUBLISHING
Lake Ann, Mich.

A D Professional Development Publishing
Lake Ann, Mich.

Khouri, Michael, D.

The power of ownership: a tale about the importance of taking control of your career and your life / Michael D. Khouri — Lake Ann, Mich. : A D Professional Development Publishing, 2007.

p. ; cm.

ISBN-13: 978-0-9796809-0-8

1. Motivation (Psychology). 2. Career Development. 3. Life change events. 4. Control (Psychology). 5. Choice (Psychology). 6. Attitude change. I. Title.

BF503 .K46 2007   2007929415
153.8—dc22   0707

Printed in the United States of America
10   9   8   7   6   5   4   3   2   1

Book design by To The Point Solutions
www.tothepointsolutions.com

To my wife, Barbara, for her love and support.
Barbara is truly a person who takes ownership in
everything she does.

To our daughters, Katie and Claire,
who have made us very proud parents.

And, to my parents, Louise and Harold, who taught me at an
early age the importance of taking ownership.

Contents

Preface

There are two constants in life that we can expect to encounter: adversity and change. They will always happen. Sometimes adversity and change come in small doses; but, there are times when they stay with us beyond the event, they are significant, and they are life-impacting.

In our business (and personal) lives, we are put in situations that ask us to make a choice, to acknowledge our preferences. We either make decisions—or they are made for us. Regardless of our behavior, we are all risk takers. We either take control or risk accepting what life offers.

We have all experienced situations where we had to make choices. In today's demanding business world, when responsibilities and competition can be overwhelming, our perspective on taking ownership has never been more crucial to our success and overall enjoyment.

The Power of Ownership is an allegory about two communities of squirrels that experience opposite results from a major storm due to their different perspectives on life. Their stories show how we must own what we decide to do—or not to do. There is no in-between in terms of decision versus non-decision.

This book is a mirror of the process people go through when facing both small and life-altering events. Its purpose is to motivate you to take charge of your career and life. If you do not—if instead you allow others to decide your path—you are taking a much greater risk.

The
Power
of
Ownership

Chapter One

PREFERENCE OR UPHEAVAL?

We are all risk takers; some make their choices
while others risk taking what comes to them.

In the small town of Preference there
resided three squirrels: Preneur, Prolific, and
Providence. They lived together because it fit their
needs. To most squirrels, Preference was nothing
more than a few large trees surrounded by burrows.
To Preneur, Prolific, and Providence, it was home.

Preneur was a tree squirrel and thrived in their
made-for-shelter homestead. He enjoyed water that
came from the tree and, with the help of Prolific,

searched for food, which consisted of nuts, seeds, and pine cones. Unlike most squirrels in the region that discarded the shells and ate only the nut meat, these two squirrels ate the husks and the nuts.

Their mission was to make this the best home that hard work could provide. Preneur, as the legal owner of the homestead was ultimately responsible for the success of the enterprise. He brought good organizational skills and energy into the relationship. He was comfortable making major decisions relative to taking the shelter to another level and making sure they always had a supply of food. Preneur was proud of their home.

Preneur involved Prolific in the decision-making process because, like Preneur, Prolific made the success of their enterprise a top priority. He, too, had a tremendous amount of energy and was execution-oriented. His major contribution, however, was the pursuit of quality and purpose. Prolific could well have been considered the force behind the enterprise. Based on the contribution each brought to its success, it was difficult to know who had legal rights to the homestead.

Prolific, like Preneur, was optimistic about life. He knew that he alone determined his own well-being. Having this kind of perspective on life allowed these squirrels to enjoy their own company as much as they enjoyed each others.

Whenever a storm rolled into town or they were attacked by a hawk or an owl, they made a point of learning everything they could from the experience so they would be better prepared the next time it happened. Because of this attitude, Preneur and Prolific were always able to work through challenging situations while gaining a little wisdom each time.

They also knew that, if necessary, they could depend on the extensive network of friends and acquaintances they had built up over the years for help.

Their friend Providence, a ground squirrel, lived in the burrow at the base of their tree. The only difference between Providence and the other two was that Providence was willing to take what life gave him. He did not ask for much, and as such, he did not expect much. He had enough shelter, food, and water to fit his needs—and that is all that mattered to him.

Whatever Providence had in life, met his vision. He was content.

15

You have brains in your head
You have feet in your shoes
You can steer yourself
Any direction you choose

DR. SEUSS (THEODOR SEUSS GEISEL)

These three optimistic and confident companions shared a common perspective on life: they recognized that they alone defined who they were and who they wanted to be. They respected each other and everyone they came in contact with. And, although these squirrels took their work seriously, they tried not to take themselves too seriously. After all, at the end of the day, life was really theater. They made a point to enjoy the show.

Even though Preneur and Prolific worked hard, they also took time to play. A day did not pass without them having fun and forgetting about the demands of hunting for food or working at improving their shelter. Providence also took time out from whatever he was doing to interact with his friends. And, sometimes, they did nothing but sit and watch the activity around them. Life was good.

A few miles away, in Upheaval, there lived three other squirrels. There was a tree squirrel named Uni, a flying squirrel named Unkno, and a ground squirrel named Untra.

Their tree and burrow was nothing special. It was what it was. It was a place to reside in the middle of Upheaval. These squirrels were not motivated to make any improvements to their home.

Uni preferred being anonymous. He did not want to be burdened with expectations he had no intention of attempting to fulfill. He had no desire to be recognized for any accomplishments. He believed setting goals was nothing more than a disaster waiting to happen.

Uni believed tragedy would occur no matter what precautions were taken and regardless of any effort given. His attitude was "Why bother in the first place?" He chose to save the energy that effort consumed and the worry that anticipation caused and just let things happen.

Everything that Uni did in life was unintentional, even though there was never any intent on his part to make it so. His lack of perspective and initiative allowed him to be the recipient of whatever crossed his path. As such, he was given the name Unintentional. Over the years, it was shortened to Uni, not intentionally, it just happened.

Uni had not looked for Upheaval; it seemed to have found him. The tree he lived in just happened to be there. One day he was tired from going nowhere and doing nothing, so he rested in the tree for no other reason than the tree was there. It was

We choose our joys and sorrows
long before we experience them.

KAHLIL GIBRAN

convenient. He stopped—and without any thought or effort—ended up staying. He was never sure why (not that he spent any time or energy wondering why).

If Uni's history is making you dizzy and confused, think how Uni felt living this existence. It was exhausting.

Unkno came by Upheaval in a different way; although like Uni, he had not been searching for Upheaval specifically, it just seemed to find him. Unkno did not know Upheaval before his arrival.

Unkno made a point to stay as clueless and unaware as he could. This took no effort; he only had to close his eyes to what was going on around him and refuse to learn anything new.

Unkno was simply not interested in knowing there may be a way to change things. He did not want to make the effort to learn of other possibilities because that could require more work than he was willing to do. He was comfortable keeping his options limited and exposing himself to as little as possible. He did not realize he did this; he just did it.

Unkno believed that disaster waited around every corner, and he was content not finding out what it might be any sooner than necessary. He wasn't against setting goals; he did not realize this option existed. He was unaware because he never sought information from others. He kept his distance from anyone who might educate him on the benefits of knowledge. Because of this seclusion and lack of effort to change, Unkno did not know what he did not know.

Anything Unkno did in life was not something he did knowingly. Things just happened to him. He did not know why and he certainly did not know how.

Unkno did not realize that his lack of initiative caused him to receive what came his way—and nothing more. As such, the name others gave him was Unknowingly. Over the years, the name was shortened to Unkno.

Untra, the third squirrel living in Upheaval, kept his nose to the ground. He was not in pursuit of anything—he simply focused on the land because it took too much effort to look up.

Unlike Uni, Untra's lack of curiosity and learning was not unintentional; in fact, it was quite intentional. He lacked the energy and dedication to do anything. And, unlike Unkno, Untra was fully aware of his lack of desire to learn. He was not trained to do anything, so he did nothing. He just went along.

Untra's expectations and goals were minimal because he was not qualified to do much. He knowingly made no effort to advance his knowledge and was content with getting by with his limited skill set. He had no desire to develop any talents that might take his abilities to a higher level. He was comfortable enough at ground level.

Untra was aware that disaster could enter his life at any time, but he did not care. Taking precautions meant he would have to learn something. He knew he would not enjoy this, so he did not bother.

Untra could have impacted his existence if he only made an effort to open his life to learning; but he refused training of any sort. As such, others called him Untrained. Over the years, his name was shortened to Untra.

Untra did not seek to live in Upheaval nor did he recognize Upheaval when he saw it. If he had taken the time to investigate, he would have known there were better places to live than Upheaval. Untra, with his untrained eye, could not tell that Upheaval was limited in what it had to offer a squirrel. He settled in Upheaval because he did not know

You may be disappointed if you fail, but you are doomed if you don't try.

BEVERLY SILLS

any better. Untra had neither the knowledge nor skill set to comprehend his lack of understanding.

Uni, Unkno, and Untra shared a common perspective on life: they did not take ownership for anything that happened to them and they were accountable to no one, including themselves. Because of this outlook, things constantly happened to them that they had no control over and, worse yet, never anticipated.

It wasn't that Uni, Unkno, and Untra did not like others, or each other; they just never took the time to contemplate the possibility. It was easier to unknowingly and unintentionally go through life and not make an effort to learn anything.

> Real knowledge is to know the extent of one's ignorance.
>
> CONFUCIUS

As a result, these three squirrels were the most pessimistic beings you could ever meet. In their opinion, nothing in life had ever gone right and there was no indication that anything on the horizon would come along to change that. There was one thing they were very good at, though. They were good prophets. They predicted that nothing would ever turn out well—and they were always right.

Unfortunately, what they did not understand was that because of their negative prophesying and lack of commitment, effort, and desire to open their eyes to their environment, they would continue to experience the same results: disaster.

Their lack of interest produced a low standard of expectation. Because life was cruel and rough, these squirrels only took one thing seriously—and that was themselves. With this kind of existence, they saw no humor in anything.

Are you wondering if these three animals at least respected each other? Don't think too hard; appreciation and respect come from getting to know someone. They had never taken the time to do this. They just happened to be drawn to the same tree and situations. They did not know why, nor did they care.

Uni, Unkno, and Untra did not interact with each other—or anyone else for that matter. They did not sit and watch the activity around them. Life was not good!

Chapter Two

THESE BIRDS HAVE A LEG UP

Always be open to new information;
Even if it is from a turkey!

As time passed, the squirrels of Preference continued to work together, building their enterprise and enjoying the fruits of their labor; while the squirrels in Upheaval lived close to each other without collaborating on any cause.

It was the middle of November and the weather in this four-season climate was finally beginning to cool as winter and all that it could bring neared.

This autumn had been different than most in

that it was warmer than usual and thoughts of snow and ice seemed like distant problems that were of no concern to some.

The squirrels of Preference, even though they enjoyed the unseasonably warm weather, knew it was only a matter of time before it would turn cold. They worked especially hard to make sure that their tree was secure and that the burrows were latched down. They knew this was their last chance to gather as much food as they could before the snow fell.

They had an efficient system in place where each squirrel had a significant role in securing the shelters and cleaning and storing the seeds and nuts they would need to sustain them in the upcoming months. It was a system that had improved dramatically over the years due to good, honest evaluation and discussion, and open minds to look at new ways of doing things.

In contrast, the squirrels in Upheaval never thought about the changing weather or made an effort to prepare for winter. For them, it might as well have been April or July. No change in seasons was going to impact their lack of desire to do any more than they had to.

There is no knowledge, no light, no wisdom that you are in posession of but what you have received it from some source.

BRIGHAM YOUNG

⤳

Uni, Unkno, and Untra continued to lie around and wander aimlessly—unknowingly and unintentionally. It did not matter to them, nor did they consider the fact that their uninterested, unaccountable approach to life caused them nothing but heartache winter after winter.

Not only did they have no system in place, they were not about to exert energy discussing and evaluating any possible plans. Their minds were closed and their eyes shut.

On this particular day, when Preference was full of excitement with accomplishment and antici-

You cannot escape the
responsibility of tomorrow
by evading it today.

ABRAHAM LINCOLN

pation of the changing season, two turkeys waddled into the area. These were not average turkeys. When these birds came near, everyone noticed. Time had served them well. They had done a good job of keeping their noses to the ground, in a positive way, and had learned much over the years.

They not only knew how to get most things done, they were also open to learning new ways that had not yet been tested. These turkeys were filled with massive amounts of knowledge. And, they had unique names that did not reflect what they looked like.

The older turkey was called Lean, though he was anything but. He was so rotund that it was hard to imagine he was not stuffed enough to make it through two winters, let alone one. Yet, Lean never took any winter for granted and always planned ahead to make sure he was able to limit the effect of the surprises that came into his life. Lean even wrote on his calendar each fall to keep a low profile, something he described as being in his "best interests".

His companion, Mean, was the most congenial and friendly turkey you would ever meet.

Although Mean was slender, he was so fit he could make an Olympic athlete green with envy. And, like Lean, Mean took nothing for granted. He, too, was a planner and prided himself on being prepared for any physical and mental test that came his way.

Lean and Mean took ownership of their lives, and as such, they felt in control, as much as two turkeys could. They also understood that no matter how much you plan, things can go wrong—whether you're a turkey or not.

> Effective leadership is not about making speeches or being liked; leadership is defined by results not attributes.
>
> PETER DRUCKER

32

Upon reaching Preference, they were quick to appreciate the upkeep of Preneur, Prolific, and Providence's small town. It was neat, finely decorated, well planned out for handling traffic of any kind, and the signage made it easy for visitors to find their way through town without needing to ask for directions.

Also it was clear to see where a hungry passerby could acquire a fine meal of fruit and nuts. Preference offered nuts with husks; nuts without husks; and plain husks, for those with a less particular preference, no pun intended.

Lean and Mean knew this enterprise meant a lot to somebody. They could see the pride of ownership. They were glad they had taken the time to stop.

Upon reaching the outside burrow of the town, they were greeted by Preneur, Prolific, and Providence, who were always willing and ready to meet with any guests who might stroll, roll, fly, crawl, or waddle into town.

Since Lean and Mean were on a specific mission this day, they quickly got through the introductions before they all huddled under the tree. Lean spoke first.

"Mean and I are making the rounds to pass on

some information that you may find useful," he stated with a serious tone. "Based on our knowledge of the region and the studies we have been doing, we believe there is a major storm coming this way that could uproot your town if it is not secure enough."

"How do you know?" asked Preneur intently and with some concern in his voice.

"There are things we always watch carefully that seem to be a precursor to these kinds of storms; and all indications are that a big one may be coming in the next week," said Lean. "We are trying to alert as many towns as we can in the next few days, before we take cover."

"How secure do you think we need to make our town?" asked Prolific. "We probably should get right to work on it," he added, before Lean or Mean could respond.

"I expect the winds to reach destructive proportions, causing much twisting and breaking of limbs and trees. Everything should be secured as tightly as possible."

"Well, we should probably get down to business and do what we need to do," said Providence. "Thanks for the warning."

We must have strong minds,
ready to accept facts as they are.

HARRY S. TRUMAN

"You are welcome," Lean and Mean answered.

The three squirrels then sat down with the turkeys and enjoyed some food and conversation. They kept the visit short because Lean and Mean had to move on. The squirrels again thanked the turkeys for the information and the two turkeys thanked the squirrels for their hospitality. It was time for Lean and Mean to depart.

Upon arriving in Upheaval, the difference between it and Preference was quickly apparent. At first Lean and Mean thought it was abandoned. No one was in sight and the place looked and smelled like an unkempt dump.

Maneuvering through the messy town was difficult because there was no signage to direct them. Travelers had better not be hungry when going through this part of the region, because not only would they be unable to locate a place to eat, they would probably be leery of eating what food was available. The squalor was appalling. Lean and Mean almost regretted their decision to stop.

But, being turkeys of high character and integrity, they believed it was their responsibility to attempt to warn anyone that lived in the area.

After determining where Uni, Unkno, and

Untra were—thanks to some heavy snoring that could be heard because of the quiet from lack of activity—Lean and Mean knocked on an opening of a tree and burrow to try to get the squirrels' attention.

The first pounding received no response; but finally, after knocking for what seemed like thirty minutes, three yawning squirrels came stumbling outside.

As he wiped the sleep from his eyes, Uni demanded loudly, "What do you two turkeys want?"

"We are sorry to have awakened you from your sleep, but we have some information that you may want to know," said Lean calmly.

"You woke us up to make us aware of something we *might* want to know?" an irritated Unkno shot back.

"There is a major storm heading this way soon. You may want to start preparing for it as quickly as you can," said Mean in a friendly tone.

"If we wanted advice on what we should work on, we certainly would not get it from a couple of turkeys," snapped Untra.

"Get out of here!" the squirrels screamed in unison at the surprised turkeys.

It requires wisdom to understand wisdom; the music is nothing if the audience is deaf.

WALTER LIPPMANN

⌣

Even though Lean and Mean had been rudely treated, they were still concerned about the safety of these lazy and irritable squirrels. But, they quickly realized that there was no way they were going to get the squirrels to listen to their message. Mean and Lean did not stay around to debate the issue, they left. As bad as they felt about the situation, they knew they could not force the squirrels to listen.

As Lean and Mean gingerly made their way through the clutter in Upheaval they rationalized that, in spite of their lack of success in this town, at least Preference had been receptive to their message—and they had made some new friends at the same time. A success ratio of one out of two is never bad, they reasoned. They decided to take the success they had in Preference, learn from the experience in Upheaval, and move on. And, that's exactly what they did.

We must accept finite disappointment, but never lose infinite hope.

MARTIN LUTHER KING, JR.

Chapter Three

A Wise Owl Gives a Hoot

Even a good system can be improved. The better you are prepared for a storm, the better your chances of weathering it.

Preneur, Prolific, and Providence were diligently working and maximizing the use of their time to be well prepared for the coming storm. Each morning they met to lay out a plan for the day. Their goal was to stabilize the tree and burrow to withstand whatever winds and precipitation the storm brought, and to gather as much food as possible in the time they had.

Preneur used his management expertise, Prolific added his unrelenting energy, and

Providence went beyond his usual just-enough-to-get-by attitude to help. The town was abuzz with more activity than normal, which was saying a lot. Thanks to the far-reaching network these diligent squirrels had developed over the years, they were able to get assistance from others in the area who were already prepared or who could fly away to another location to escape the worst of the storm. The three residents of Preference were appreciative of the help and they assigned tasks to the volunteers as quickly as offers were made.

The squirrels soon realized they had a problem: they were lacking consistency in the tasks and if they continued in this fashion, they would not gather enough food or prepare their tree and burrow well enough. Time and energy was being wasted. The results could be better, but how?

One morning while discussing what needed to be accomplished, they were suddenly interrupted by an owl's repeated hooting. Normally owls are a natural enemy of squirrels, but Champion was not only a friend; she was a well-educated and auspicious bird.

"I believe we have a distinguished guest in our presence," said Preneur to his companions.

One of the tests of leadership is
the ability to recognize a problem
before it becomes an emergency.

ARNOLD GLASGOW

"Welcome, Champion. We are pleased to have you join us this morning."

"Thank you, Preneur," said Champion.

"What brings you here?" Prolific asked.

"I heard of the coming storm from Lean and Mean, and figured that with the limited time you have to gather food and materials, consistency of operation and efficiency might be important to you."

"What a great sense of timing," replied Providence. "Even though we have always thought ourselves to be efficient, it would sure be great to hear any suggestions you have on how to reduce the variation results of our system."

"With time running out, it would be most helpful if we could reduce the number of defects through a better, fine-tuned process. The floor is yours, Champion," Preneur added.

Champion went through a quick indoctrination of a program to help the group identify what was causing time costly deviations along with an action plan to reduce the errors.

With Champion's expertise from years of teaching and implementation, the town of Preference was able to make tremendous strides in improving its results. Soon they were getting more seeds and nuts cleaned and stored, and the process of improving the shelter was more efficient.

Once Champion could see that the group had taken its success to a higher level and she was confident they would finish the work before the storm arrived, she said her good-byes.

Thanks to Champion, Preneur, Prolific, and Providence had not only been introduced to a new operational program, they had also learned a new term. *Six-Sigma* would forever be ingrained in their management processes.

Leaving Preference with a feeling of accomplishment and satisfaction from being able to help the squirrels, who she liked and respected, Champion moved on to her next destination.

Upon reaching Upheaval, it soon became clear that getting the inhabitants to listen to her would be a challenge. Champion had never seen so much clutter and disorganization. Furthermore, where were the residents? After flying from tree to tree to no avail, and hooting as loudly as she could for what seemed like an hour, Champion finally saw two squirrels wobbling out of a tree and another one climbing out of the burrow below.

The genius of a good leader is to leave behind him a situation which common sense, without the grace of genius, can deal with successfully.

WALTER LIPPMANN

It seemed she had woken them from a deep sleep, as they all looked groggy and grumpy. Champion realized they were irritated the minute she heard them scream in unison, "Who in the %@*^&% is making all that $%#@&* noise?!"

"Sorry," said Champion apologetically, "but there is a major storm coming this way and I thought you might be able to use my expertise."

"I certainly hope you did not intentionally make this unsolicited, unwanted, and unwarranted visit to Upheaval, because we are not interested!" screamed Uni.

"You know, two turkeys waddled into town a few days ago to warn us of some stinking storm," Unkno snorted. "It was bad enough when they interrupted us with nonsense they know nothing about—and now you expect us to believe you, another worthless bird who probably doesn't know any more than a turkey?" he added with irritation in his voice.

"I was just in Preference," Champion explained, "and was able to introduce a new concept that even they, with their fine enterprise and organization, felt would be helpful in improving their ability to prepare for the storm."

"If we were interested in any training, we'd ask for it. Let me assure you, we are *not* interested in any stinking training—and if we were, the last place we'd get it from is a stupid bird," screamed Untra.

"Well, I'm sorry you feel that way," Champion calmly replied. "I do believe Upheaval could use my Six-Sigma concept; even more so than Preference."

"We don't want your *help* . . . we don't want your *Six* . . . and we most certainly don't want your *Sigma*!" the squirrels shouted.

"Well," said Champion, "it is obvious you are in no position to weather out the coming storm. I hope you will reconsider before it is too late. I do wish you well. Good-bye."

Being a wise owl, Champion was able to put this disturbing episode into perspective as she left Upheaval. She assured herself that the squirrels had been given a choice. And, she was sure this was not the first time their lack of training caused them to not understand the importance of perpetual growth and development. Actually, it may have been the one time in their lives when their decision—or lack of decision—was not unintentionally based.

Never attribute to malice that which can be adequately explained by stupidity.

ANON

As she exited the sorry town, Champion knew she had done the best she could with what she had to work with. And, most importantly, she cared. Yes, indeed, she gave a hoot.

Plus, her purpose had not been wasted. Preference had an excellent chance of surviving the storm. The open perspective of Preneur, Prolific, and Providence was clearly going to produce better results than the closed mindedness she had witnessed in Upheaval.

Chapter Four

Preservation or Not

Even a good plan should have a backup.

One day after Champion's visit to Preference and Upheaval, three squirrels from the town of Preservation visited. Knowing that this region was positioned in the eye of the coming storm, these goodwill ambassadors, whose town was safely located outside the projected path of the storm, had come to offer a proposal.

The trio consisted of a tree squirrel named Anticipation, a flying squirrel named Respond, and a ground squirrel named Security. They were long-time friends who not only thought highly of each other, but also felt a certain alignment in terms of their beliefs. They worked well together and had been successful in their common pursuit of enjoying life.

Anticipate, the elder statesman, had taken on a leadership role for the group. Respond, who was execution-oriented and knew what it took to bring a plan to closure, was always ready and able to lead them through any challenge. Security was perceptive and understood what they were trying to accomplish. He added purpose to any endeavor.

Anticipate, Respond, and Security had heard of the adventures of Lean and Mean and Champion in their efforts to assist the towns of Preference and Upheaval. They knew that not everyone shared their beliefs and would accept the value of their proposal.

It did not matter to these goodwill ambassadors that their trip may fail. What was important to them is that they were doing everything in their power to succeed. They knew that helping others had its limitations and that real empowerment was something that one could only give to oneself.

Action may not always bring
happiness; but there is no
happiness without action.

BENJAMIN DISRAELI

The discipline you learn and character you build from setting and achieving a goal can be more valuable than the achievement of the goal itself.

BO BENNETT

Upon reaching Preference, they too were impressed with not only the beauty but also the ownership these residents displayed. It was a town that surely had a history of strategic planning, and the squirrels' ability to put actions to their plans had produced some admirable results. There was no doubt that Preneur, Prolific, and Providence knew purpose and where its impetus came from.

Knowing Preference was inhabited by only three squirrels, it was surprising and impressive to see the number of other animals that were busily working together, clearly on a dedicated mission. It was obvious that these three squirrels had not only developed a significant network, but they were also putting it to use.

While walking through town, Anticipate, Respond, and Security were greeted with smiles. They stopped one of the busy workers to ask where the three residents could be found. They were directed to the main tree and burrow in the center of town.

Sure enough, when they reached the location, Preneur, Prolific, and Providence were meeting with a group of workers to discuss the status of their

THE POWER OF OWNERSHIP

assigned areas and the results to date. Listening to them talk gave Anticipate, Respond, and Security the same exhilaration as a classical music enthusiast might get from listening to *The Flight of the Bumblebee*.

Not wanting to interrupt, but knowing they should, the three visitors walked up to the group. "We are sorry to break up this fine meeting, but we have a proposal we want you to consider. May we talk?" said Anticipate.

The three residents of Preference quickly turned around to acknowledge the guests.

"Why certainly," said Preneur. "We did not realize you were here. Sorry. We were focused on our urgent project. These are my colleagues, Prolific and Providence. We are pleased to meet you. Welcome to our humble town."

"Thank you," said Respond. "These are my colleagues, Anticipate and Security," he added.

"We understand there is a storm coming and we would like to offer our assistance—just in case it should become necessary," Security interjected.

"It is our belief that because of all the hard work everyone has contributed over the last few days, including Champion, whose program we implemented, we should be okay," replied Prolific. "But, we are always open to new ideas or possibilities," he added.

"In the chance that all your preparations are not enough to save your town from the storm, we want to let you know that you are welcome to take up residence with us in Preservation," Anticipate said.

Even though Preneur, Prolific, and Providence were confident they had taken the proper precautions to withstand any kind of storm, they were profoundly overwhelmed at the kindness and hospitality of the three visitors.

"Thank you very much. We will inject your offer into our game plan; and, if by chance, all this preparation does not let us survive the storm, we will visit Preservation and consider your offer," said Preneur.

Prolific and Providence quickly agreed with Preneur and gave their acceptance to this backup plan.

Preneur, Prolific, and Providence ended their meeting and invited the kind visitors to join them for a splendid dinner of seasoned fruit and nuts. The visitors were happy to take a short rest and eat before they continued on their journey.

After dinner, the residents of Preference and their visitors exchanged pleasantries. Then it was time for Anticipate, Respond, and Security to depart.

It had been an enjoyable experience for them and they felt accomplished as they made their way toward Upheaval. It was their belief that Preference would likely survive the storm as its residents had done a good job of strategic planning and they were organized and committed in their execution.

What really impressed the three visitors, though, was the way Preneur, Prolific, and Providence had taken ownership of a pending problem. They were depending on the most impacting resource to combat this major challenge: themselves.

Upon reaching the outskirts of Upheaval, Anticipate, Respond, and Security were greeted by disarray and unsettling quiet. Not only was there no activity, but a major basic cleanup would have to occur first. One thing was clear: these residents

Gratitude is not only the greatest of virtues, but the parent of all others.

SIR WINSTON CHURCHILL

were not ready for the pending storm. Furthermore, it appeared as though they did not care.

The trio from Preservation was not strangers to planning, tough execution, and taking charge—they most certainly would not back away from this challenge. Nothing would change their approach and perspective.

They soon decided that the bottom line on this situation was that the residents of Upheaval would have to join them immediately in Preservation. Time had run out for Upheaval. It was hard to imagine that anyone would admit they owned the place.

Anticipate, Respond, and Security continued to traverse the cluttered paths of Upheaval in an attempt to locate any residents. Every step magnified the sense of urgency. The faster they found these residents, the better for all concerned.

When they reached the middle of town, where the main tree was located, they noticed a burrow that was almost entirely covered with nut husks and leaves. As they stopped to take in the eyesore, they spotted three squirrels. One was hanging on a branch by his leg—it appeared to have unintentionally gotten caught. A second was at the bottom of the tree, sucking on a rock they were sure it had mistaken for a nut. The third squirrel was lying on a leaf with his feet in the air. It was hard to tell if he was trying to move the leaf or if he was attempting to scratch an itchy back.

Two things were clear to the goodwill ambassadors: these squirrels were not engaged, and there certainly was no sense of urgency here.

"*What* is going on here?" Anticipate shouted. "Don't you realize a major storm is headed this way?"

"You're as bad as those two turkeys that waddled in here," Unkno screamed back at Anticipate. "If a stupid storm is coming, not only do we not want to know about it, we don't care to know about it."

"*Where* is your sense of engagement?" an exasperated Respond exclaimed, his voice cracking from the frustration of what he was witnessing.

"We're not qualified to fight a storm, nor do we have any desire to learn what it might take," shouted Untra. "We'll get by, and this won't be the first or the last storm we ever see," he added.

"*How* could you just leave your fate to others?" screamed Security. "Where is your sense of self?"

"What a bunch of garbage," yelled Uni. "If a

storm is going to come, it's going to come; anything we do or don't do is not going to stop it from coming! Why waste energy we don't have?" he added.

It was uncommon for Anticipate, Respond, and Security to lose their cool, but the indifference and lack of initiative was something that was foreign to them—they had never seen it on such a shockingly high scale.

These squirrels of Upheaval were definitely not prepared for any storm. It was obvious they needed refuge quickly. In spite of the awful hospitality, they would still make their offer to these head-in-the-sand squirrels.

"It is clear to us that you have no expectations one way or another in regards to this upcoming storm," Anticipate calmly stated. "We have made preparations for you to join us in Preservation, to ride out the storm safely," he added.

"No way are you going to get us to intention-ally uproot ourselves and go to any Preservation," Uni said.

"We don't know anything about Preservation," added Unkno.

"And we don't care to learn anything about Preservation," Untra shouted.

It was evident to the visitors that they had no chance of getting through to these ornery, uninterested, and unwilling squirrels. It was time to leave.

As the three visitors departed Upheaval, they were concerned that the residents of this small, messy place would not survive. But, there was nothing they could do. The shear disregard of the squirrels in Upheaval was the worst that Anticipate, Respond, and Security had ever experienced.

It was hard for them to believe the total lack of ownership the residents of Upheaval had exhibited. It was bad enough that the residents were reluctant to even consider using any outside resources; but, what was more telling was their refusal to use themselves.

The difference between a
successful person and others
is not a lack of strength, not a
lack of knowledge, but rather
a lack of will.

VINCE LOMBARDI

Chapter Five

Vision by Preference

Strategic planning, execution, and perspective do not assure success; but they do improve your chances.

Back in Preference, the activity was like that in a beehive on a warm summer day. Every participant was doing his or her part to make sure that their combined efforts would result in success. The decision to stay had been a difficult one and was not made lightly. The residents and their friends knew that a positive outcome required a dedicated team effort. That alone would have a great impact on the end result.

The most difficult thing is the
decision to act, the rest is merely
tenacity. The fears are paper tigers.
You can do anything you decide
to do. You can act to change
and control your life; and the
procedure, the process is its
own reward.

ROBYN DAVIDSON

It would have been easier for Preneur, Prolific, and Providence to accept the offer made by Anticipate, Respond, and Security; but it was not in their makeup to take the first easy way out to a problem—no matter how challenging. The fact that they had a different vision not only increased their determination, it gave them the fortitude to combat obstacles and surprises.

Preneur, Prolific, and Providence were not foolish enough to think that strategic planning, execution, and fine-tuning along the way would automatically make them invincible. What they did know was that taking ownership put them in a position where they could control their destiny. They understood that their pro-active perspective put them in a situation where they would always, at the very least, learn from any experience. As a result, they would be in a better position for any future challenges; if they should fail at this one.

No matter what happened, they were in a position to succeed, and the path they took would give them something that was important to have in life: the satisfaction of purpose.

Purpose may not be enough to make it through this storm; but, with purpose, they knew that their enjoyment would not be measured based on one event. They were long-term thinkers. The idea was to enjoy the ride. To them, life was a marathon; it was not defined entirely by today's challenges. There was tomorrow, the next day, and the many other days that would follow.

They took pleasure in today, but it was tomorrow that always put today into perspective for them. This is where their persistence and determination was rooted. If they failed today, they could look in the mirror and know they gave their best and that today's failure would not be tomorrow's as long as they learned from today. For now, they had to make sure they had done everything they needed to do to be ready to face the storm.

> The manner in which one endures what must be endured is more important than the thing that must be endured.
>
> DEAN ACHESON

If we don't change, we don't grow.
If we don't grow, we aren't really
living.

GAIL SHEEHY

Before sending their friends back to their homes, Preneur, Prolific, and Providence made a circle around the town to review the strength of the landscape and to make sure the infrastructure was as stable as it could be. They evaluated the brush and branches, and checked the wood piles that would be the first line of defense from the storm. It was clear that the assistance they had received from their friends had produced some good results.

They also realized the gain they had received from implementing the Six-Sigma program that Champion had introduced. This program had definitely been worth every minute they had taken to understand it. Being open to new ideas, no matter how efficient they had been without the program, had paid tremendous dividends.

These three squirrels had always believed that for any enterprise to be successful and to prosper over the long haul it had to continually be open to improvement and change. They knew that the quickest way to doom was to perpetually stay the same while everything around changed.

There was still a bit more work to do, but not much. Everyone gathered around to receive their final assignments. These were small tasks—a few alterations on the shelter and some precautionary additions to the food inventory—then, they would be ready.

They said farewell and thank you to everyone who had come to help. After storing the last nut and piece of fruit, and making a final adjustment to the shelter, the three residents huddled one more time to review the status of their situation.

Preneur went through the action list one item at a time, while Prolific and Providence checked the status of each task. Once he reached the end of the list and they were comfortable with total completion, they shook hands and congratulated each other on a job well done. They did not know if what had been accomplished would stand up to the power of the coming storm without fail; but they were certain they had done everything possible to put them in a position to withstand it.

And, they knew there was the option of riding out the storm in Preservation. It was comforting and wise to have an alternate plan. They made their way into the shelter. The storm would soon arrive.

The mighty oak was once a little nut that stood its ground.

ANON

Chapter Six

IGNORANCE IS NOT BLISS

Having no plan is actually a plan;
It's just not a good one.

It was a quiet week in Upheaval, like all others before it—except, of course, for the unexpected visitors—and that commotion had been forced upon Uni, Unkno, and Untra. Upheaval was the epitome of inactivity, inefficiency, and obliviousness. The place was a mess, and it did not appear there was any chance for things to improve. Uni, Unkno, and Untra were doing what they did best—absolutely nothing.

The only movement was the occasional fall of a leaf or a branch. Nowhere was there evidence that any activity had taken place. The three residents were pretty much in the same position they had been since Anticipate, Respond, and Security's visit.

Upheaval was an accident waiting to happen —well, let me correct that, the accident had already happened. What was not obvious, yet, is what would occur due to the resident's continued course of inaction.

In actuality, the lack of effort on the part of these squirrels and their refusal to even acknowledge the oncoming storm was a decision. There may not have been a plan or an approach to a solution, but there had been a direction—and that direction was to do nothing. And that, in and of itself, was a decision.

> We can try to avoid making choices by doing nothing, but even that is a decision.
>
> GARY COLLINS

Furthermore, Uni, Unkno, and Untra were risk takers. They were taking the risk that their perspective (or lack of), their effort (or lack of), and their vision (or lack of), would not be detrimental.

Everyone is a risk taker. The only difference between those that take control and those that choose not to take control is who or what determines their fate. Those who take control put fate in their own hands, whereas those who do not take control leave their fate for others and/or events to decide.

What most puzzled everyone who came in contact with Uni, Unkno, and Untra is their refusal to take shelter in Preservation. The truth is, Uni, Unkno, and Untra could not see the difference between Upheaval and Preservation! Keeping their eyes shut and their minds closed did not allow them to make a distinction.

Their lack of concern was not rooted in being strong or tough or a belief in their invincibility. On the contrary. It was a weakness that caused them to ignore everything that happened to them and around them.

Uni, Unkno, and Untra not only had no backup plan; they had no plan at all, period. There

The purpose of life is
a life of purpose.

ROBERT BYRNE

was no ownership. They did not understand or care that their destiny was something they could impact. They would never be in a better position as a result of learning from a mistake or bad experience. They were clearly in the repeat business.

Success meant nothing to them, and enjoyment was something that had never been considered. There was no purpose—and there would be no effort to find it.

Uni, Unkno, and Untra saw no difference between today and tomorrow. They were not long-term (or short-term) thinkers; the results had always been the same, so why bother?

They had no network. There was no gathering of friends or meetings about how to prepare for the storm. There was no concern about finishing tasks, as none had been started. There was no action list to be checked. Things were as they had been from the first announcement of the coming storm. Change was not an issue; there was no course to change.

Years ago, there was a rumor that the three residents of Upheaval had, at one time, made an effort. According to the story, the squirrels had tried three times to create a working enterprise and to establish an organized approach for gathering food. According to credible sources, because their efforts resulted in failure each time, the squirrels came to the conclusion that it did not matter if they tried or not. So, they gave up.

There were two points that Uni, Unkno, and Untra did not realize during these times of failure. First, in order to achieve success, one must take ownership. Secondly, if you learn from your mistakes, you reduce the chances of repetition, which eventually will produce successful results.

Persistence and staying focused were not qualities these squirrels excelled in; so they stopped trying.

In the distance, the winds of the storm were beginning to blow. The storm would be here soon.

Apathy is a sort of living oblivion.

HORACE GREELEY

Chapter Seven

ADVERSITY STRIKES ALL

The question isn't if we will face adversity in our lives; rather it is how will we face adversity when it comes?

By midday, clouds were overhead and the morning's light breeze had intensified to a menacing howl. The rain, which started as a fine drizzle, was coming down in sheets. The sky darkened. By mid-afternoon it was as black as any night. It was looking more and more like a storm these parts had never seen.

It seemed as if the wind and rain were trying to out-do the other. Would the rain come down harder than the wind blew or would the wind blow harder

Adversity is the first path to truth.

LORD GEORGE GORDON BYRON

than the rain fell? The trees and burrows in Preference and Upheaval could only hope that the battle for supremacy would end and no winner would be declared. The land was certainly not going to take sides. It did not want to get on the bad side of either force.

As leaves dropped, branches broke off, and the trees bent, it was clear that this was not an ordinary rainstorm.

Preneur and Prolific snuggled inside the main tree and listened to the sounds of Mother Nature's fury. Down below, in the burrow, Providence lie quietly as he felt the roots straining to keep the tree upright. They realized quickly that the turkeys had not underestimated the fury of this storm.

As they all huddled inside, listening to the pounding rain and massive winds that were playing havoc on their enterprise, they noted that there was no loose debris hitting their tree and burrow. This told them that they had done a good job of stabilizing the infrastructure. As bad as things were, it could have been worse.

They were also comforted to know they had stocked the pantry well. Even though they were being held hostage in their own home, it would

Pain is inevitable; suffering is optional.

HINDU SPIRITUAL

have been worse if they had not stored enough food. They would be able to ride out the storm and eat as they had on any other day, thanks to their preparation.

Meanwhile, in Upheaval, the storm was having a different effect. Branches and sticks and nuts and husks and stones—anything not secured—were flying through the air like missiles. It was like taking refuge in a popcorn maker that was on high. The constant barrage of debris was so fast and furious it caused a clutter in the air not ever witnessed before. It was like a sandstorm in the desert; but instead of only sand swirling around, the air was thick with stones, sticks, branches, nuts, dirt, and such.

As a result of different attitudes, the two communities were experiencing diverse impacts from the same storm. Because Preference had bolted everything down and had a secure infrastructure, the only thing blowing through the air was leaves. Upheaval's lack of effort resulted in what looked like a major bombing assault from the sky. It was a confrontation that Upheaval was losing badly.

Even though Uni, Unkno, and Untra had taken cover in the main tree and burrow, it was evident

Challenges are what make life interesting; overcoming them is what makes life meaningful.

JOSHUA J. MARINE

that the shelter was not going to survive the continual bombardment. The tree was going to succumb to the wind and topple, and Untra's burrow was not going to withstand the constant beating.

It was late afternoon when the howling winds and pounding rain reached the peak of their fury. Suddenly, the roots of the tree were yanked violently from the ground and the covering of the burrow was leveled, causing the opening to disappear.

Joining the flotsam in the air were three squirrels at the mercy of the furious wind. Upheaval had been leveled beyond recognition and its inhabitants were on their way to lands unknown, at the dictates of a storm that would release them when it was good and ready.

Life is a maze in which we take the wrong turn before we have learnt to walk.

CYRIL CONNOLLY

Chapter Eight

LOST IN UPHEAVAL

The distance between upheaval and preservation
is not far; it's only a matter of preference.

The day after the storm ravished its way
through the region, all was calm in Preference;
while Upheaval was chaotically and profoundly
void. These two towns, which had been beaten and
battered by the same unrelenting storm, experienced extremely different results.

In Preference, the three triumphant residents
took a victorious stroll through town, admiring the
still standing infrastructure. The land was riddled
with leaves that had blown off the trees, but that
was to be expected.

Preneur, Prolific, and Providence were pleased with their accomplishment. They knew that the preparation, hard work of many, and trying new approaches had created this success. Although there were moments during the storm when they doubted if their town would weather the onslaught, they remained confident and steadfast in the plan they had set in place. Their determination and convictions did not betray them.

They thought about their friends who had worked so hard to help them prepare for the storm, and how the visits by the two turkeys, the wise owl, and the three residents of Preservation had played a part in their success.

The two turkeys warned them that the storm was going to be brutal, and they were right. The wise owl gave them a program she thought could improve the quality of their systems, and Six-Sigma had aided them in their survival. And, the three residents of Preservation offered them refuge as a backup, if needed, and that had given them solace.

Success did not make them arrogant. If anything, they were humbled because they knew that without effort, dedication, execution, and vision they could be looking at a different situation.

Never be bullied into silence.
Never allow yourself to be made
a victim. Accept no one's
definition of your life;
define yourself.

HARVEY FIERSTEIN

With the help of their network of friends they had done what was necessary and their vision of a long-term growing, prosperous, and stable community had passed the latest test. They also knew that their ability to survive and thrive through this storm did not automatically assure success the next time.

This experience was added to previous ones, and gave them the confidence and conviction to pursue their vision.

Preneur, Prolific, and Providence would now take a little time to enjoy the fruits of their philosophy, which was built on an ability to anticipate, respond, and execute plans to meet any challenge. They knew that the only security in life one has is the security one gives to oneself.

⌒

Upheaval existed no more.

As the storm subsided, it dropped Uni, Unkno, and Untra on the outskirts of a town that they never could have found on their own. This town was

Utopia. The landscape was mesmerizing and the abundance of fruit and nuts and other fine delicacies was enough to make a squirrel's mouth pucker at the sight. There was a tranquil brook full of fish, and frogs and birds croaking and singing nearby.

Utopia offered the ultimate life. It was the peak. It was the mountaintop that many before had proclaimed as their desired destination.

As Uni, Unkno, and Untra slowly and tenderly picked themselves up from what had been a most unpleasant drop, they shook their heads and jerkily stood on all fours. Flying that long in the storm with their eyes closed resulted in a landing they had neither sought nor expected.

As they looked around, they were unsure what they were seeing. Some things, however, were clear: Uni had not intentionally sought out this place, Unkno had not knowingly sought out this area, and Untra certainly had not learned of this region.

The one thing they concluded individually, because there was no discussion, was that they were no longer in Upheaval. So, without any assessment of where they had arrived or what this new place had to offer, they walked away from the town—without any destination in mind.

These squirrels did not realize how close to Utopia they were. A major catastrophe had taken them from the depths of Upheaval to the edge of Utopia—and they wasted the opportunity.

Instead, Uni, Unkno, and Untra blindly staggered away from Utopia, with no destination in mind and no idea when they might get there. Only one thing was certain at this juncture: without any set destination, their chances of finding Upheaval were slim—but the likelihood of Upheaval finding them was a given.

As anyone who has ever lived in turmoil and chaos knows, Upheaval is not really a place—it is a result.

> It is by going down into the abyss that we recover the treasures of life. Where you stumble, there lies your treasure.
>
> JOSEPH CAMPBELL

ABOUT THE AUTHOR

 **Michael D. Khouri** is president of MDK Business Solutions, a Professional Development and Management Consulting Business. His motivational presentations to employees in many different industries, centering on the power of taking ownership, inspire people to take control of their lives and get the most out of everything they do—both personally and professionally.

Michael has thirty-two years of management experience in wireless, broadcast television, publishing, manufacturing, financial services, and retail. He has also worked as a college instructor, management consultant, and entrepreneur.

States he has managed in include Alaska, California, Illinois, and Michigan.

He can be reached at:

mkhouri@mdkbusinesssolutions.com

Professional Development & Motivational Presentations

Michael Khouri is available to present professional development training and motivational speeches to national, regional, and small local businesses on a variety of topics specifically geared to each particular business and industry. The impact of professional and personal ownership are at the core of each of his messages to owners, managers, and staff.

Listed below are a few of the presentations he has created; however, he will tailor a message to meet your company's specific needs:

15 Ways to Succeed in Sales

15 Ways to Excel at Customer Service

15 Ways to be in Control and Get the Most out of Work-Home-Health-Self

Delivering Exceptional Customer Service

Sales-Building Relationships

Keys to Management Success

Change & Challenge

How to Create a Good Work Environment

Creating Self-Initiated Accountability

Taking Control of Career & Life

Respect—Benefits & Impact to Business Success

Balance

The Impact of a Positive Perspective

Teamwork

Integrity

Building Bridges

Vision

Security Comes From Within

mdkbusinesssolutions.com
mkhouri@mdkbusinesssolutions.com